"Mastering the Subconscious Mind: Reprogram Your Life for Success"

Contents

Presentation 3

The Science Behind the Psyche 6

Releasing the Force of the Inner mind 12

Pragmatic Utilizations of Subliminal Power 19

Subliminal and Profound Wellbeing 29

Dreams and the Psyche 40

Instruments and Strategies to Bridle the Inner mind 52

Contextual investigations and Genuine Models 69

Challenges in Working with the Psyche 83

End 99

Presentation
What is the Psyche Brain?

The psyche mind is a strong and baffling piece of our psychological cycles that works underneath the outer layer of cognizant mindfulness. It is the archive of our recollections, propensities, convictions, and feelings, molding how we see the world and answer it. Dissimilar to the cognizant brain, which handles legitimate thinking and navigation, the psyche works consequently, affecting way of behaving and thought designs without us in any event, acknowledging it.

The Job of the Subliminal in Day to day existence

The psyche mind oversees quite a bit of our day to day exercises, from cleaning our teeth to driving a vehicle on autopilot. It goes about as a psychological autopilot, handling immense measures of data rapidly and effectively. More than that, it fills in as the motor behind our imagination, instinct, and profound reactions. Whether it's our internal discourse, routine ways of behaving, or intuitive responses, the psyche mind is continually working, affecting each part of our lives.

By figuring out how to access and saddle the force of the psyche, we can open boundless potential, conquer difficulties, and make enduring positive changes in our lives. This excursion starts with understanding how the inner mind works and how it interfaces with our cognizant considerations and activities.

The Science Behind the Psyche
How the Cerebrum Cycles Data

The human mind is a perplexing organ that processes immense measures of data consistently. While the cognizant psyche is restricted in its ability to zero in on a couple of undertakings all at once, the psyche works on a lot bigger scope, overseeing complex capabilities like directing internal heat level, breathing, and, surprisingly, unobtrusive profound signals. The psyche processes data in equal, guaranteeing that constant ways of behaving and robotized reactions are flawlessly coordinated into day to day existence.

Research recommends that up to 95% of our viewpoints, feelings, and activities are affected by the psyche, making it the stalwart behind the vast majority of what we do and feel. Understanding this handling power assists us with valuing its true capacity for change and development.

Cognizant versus Subliminal: Key Contrasts

The cognizant and subliminal personalities contrast in their jobs and limits:

Cognizant Psyche: Insightful, consistent, intentional, and centered. It handles present mindfulness, independent direction, and thinking.

Subliminal Brain: Natural, close to home, routine, and programmed. It stores recollections, convictions, and previous encounters that shape our ways of behaving.

While the cognizant psyche settles on quick choices, the inner mind resembles a huge data set, impacting those choices in view of put away examples and molding.

Brain adaptability and the Force of Reinventing

Brain adaptability alludes to the cerebrum's capacity to revamp itself by framing new brain associations over the course of life. This peculiarity is the establishment for reinventing the psyche mind. Rehashed contemplations, feelings, or ways of behaving make and fortify brain connections, successfully programming the inner mind.

For instance, reliably envisioning achievement or rehearsing positive attestations can modify subliminal convictions, prompting unmistakable makes progress with in propensities and results. In like manner, recognizing and tending to negative idea examples can debilitate pointless brain processes, accounting for better ones.

Brainwaves and Subliminal Access

Different brainwave frequencies assume a vital part in getting to the psyche mind:

Beta Waves (14-30 Hz): Related with cognizant concentration and readiness.

Alpha Waves (7-14 Hz): Connected to unwinding and light reflection, ideal for associating with the inner mind.

Theta Waves (4-7 Hz): Predominant during profound reflection, entrancing, and the fantasy state, giving the most immediate admittance to the psyche.

Delta Waves (0.5-4 Hz): Present during profound rest, where the psyche mind processes and incorporates data.

Understanding these brainwave states can assist us with purposefully taking advantage of the inner mind, empowering development and change.

Releasing the Force of the Inner mind

The Effect of Considerations and Convictions

Our psyche mind works to a great extent founded on the considerations and convictions it has retained, whether positive or negative. These incorporated examples shape how we see ourselves and our general surroundings. For example, a conviction, for example, "I'm not sufficient" can restrict self-improvement, while enabling convictions like "I can accomplish anything I put my energy into" can push us forward.

To release the force of the psyche, it's pivotal to intentionally supplant restricting convictions with engaging ones. By reliably taking care of the subliminal with positive considerations, we can reinvent it to line up with our objectives and desires.

Perception Procedures

Perception is an integral asset to impact the psyche mind. By distinctively envisioning an ideal result, complete with tactile subtleties and feelings, we can "stunt" the subliminal into accepting the result is genuine. This actuates the subliminal to pursue showing that reality.

For instance:

Competitors use representation to practice winning exhibitions intellectually.

Experts envision fruitful introductions or discussions to support certainty.

Ventures for powerful representation:

Shut your eyes and unwind.

Envision your objective as though it's now accomplished.

Connect every one of your faculties to make the vision as genuine as could really be expected.

Feel the feelings related with accomplishing your objective (happiness, pride, fulfillment).

Attestations: Revamping Mental Pathways

Assertions are positive articulations that, when rehashed reliably, can reshape subliminal convictions. These assertions work by supplanting negative idea designs with enabling ones, making new brain processes in the cerebrum.

Instances of attestations:

"I'm sure and fit for accomplishing my objectives."

"Overflow streams into my life easily."

"I deserve love and achievement."

To boost their adequacy:

Utilize current state (e.g., "I'm" rather than "I will be").

Rehash assertions everyday, particularly during loosened up states like early morning or before rest.

Have confidence in the reality of the assertions, regardless of whether they feel optimistic at first.

Reiteration and Propensity Arrangement

The psyche mind flourishes with redundancy. Rehashing positive considerations, activities, or ways of behaving supports new propensities after some time. This standard applies to anything from mastering another expertise to embracing a better way of life. The more reliable the redundancy, the more grounded the psyche "programming."

Appreciation and Profound States

Appreciation is a high-recurrence feeling that straightforwardly influences the psyche mind. By zeroing in on what we're thankful for, we shift our mentality toward overflow and energy, which lines up with the subliminal's normal propensities.

Day to day appreciation rehearses, such as journaling or reflecting on things you appreciate, make a positive criticism circle in the psyche, empowering it to search out additional open doors for happiness and achievement.

Relinquishing Opposition

Once in a while, the cognizant psyche opposes changes to subliminal programming because of dread or uncertainty. Strategies like care and reflection can assist with calming the cognizant psyche, making a reasonable pathway to the inner mind. By relinquishing opposition and embracing transparency, we make space for change and development.

Pragmatic Utilizations of Subliminal Power

Accomplishing Individual Objectives

The psyche mind is instrumental in accomplishing individual objectives by adjusting your inward convictions and propensities to your targets. By programming the subliminal to zero in on progress, you enact its tremendous ability to direct your activities toward wanted results.

Moves toward Apply Subliminal Capacity to Objectives:

Put forth Clear and Explicit Objectives: Characterize what you need with accuracy (e.g., "I need to acquire $10,000 in a half year" rather than "I need to get more cash-flow").

Envision the Result: Invest energy every day envisioning yourself accomplishing the objective with every one of the feelings and tactile subtleties.

Rehash Positive Attestations: Build up your trust in accomplishing the objective by rehashing proclamations like, "I'm equipped for arriving at my monetary targets."

Trust the Cycle: Keep away from overanalyzing or questioning yourself — let the psyche work behind the scenes to direct open doors and choices.

Beating Fears and Restricting Convictions

Many feelings of dread and deliberate restrictions originate from subliminal programming. By tending to these secret convictions, you can defeat obstructions that keep you down.

Procedures to Conquer Restricting Convictions:

Distinguish the Trepidation: Perceive the foundation of the restricting conviction (e.g., feeling of dread toward disappointment, dismissal, or insufficiency).

Challenge Negative Convictions: Supplant considerations like "I can't do this" with enabling options like "I'm proficient and learning consistently."

Practice Openness: Slowly confront your feelings of trepidation in a controlled manner to desensitize your subliminal to them.

Use Spellbinding or Directed Contemplation: These instruments can help rethink firmly established fears and supplant them with positive convictions.

Upgrading Imagination and Critical thinking

The psyche mind is a wellspring of innovativeness, frequently giving arrangements when the cognizant brain is very still. This is the reason "epiphanies" frequently happen during exercises like showering, strolling, or thinking.

Ways Of supporting Imagination with the Inner mind:

Dream Journaling: Keep a note pad by your bed to catch imaginative thoughts that arise during dreams.

Hatching Periods: Step away from an issue and let your inner mind process it. Frequently, the arrangement will arise unexpectedly.

Perception for Imagination: Envision yourself in imaginative situations to animate groundbreaking thoughts.

Freewriting or Psyche Planning: Let your subliminal considerations stream uninhibitedly without judgment to open new viewpoints.

Building Positive Propensities

The psyche assumes a key part in propensity development. By purposefully making positive propensities, you can reconstruct your subliminal to help a better and more useful way of life.

Moves toward Fabricate Positive Propensities:

Begin Little: Spotlight on each propensity in turn, like drinking more water or contemplating for 5 minutes day to day.

Use Triggers: Match new propensities with existing ones, such as contemplating just subsequent to cleaning your teeth.

Build up Through Reiteration: The more reliably you pursue the routine, the more imbued it becomes in your psyche.

Reward Yourself: Celebrate little wins to build up the way of behaving.

Further developing Connections

Subliminal convictions vigorously impact how we associate with others. By becoming mindful of stowed away predispositions or examples, you can further develop correspondence, compassion, and association.

Procedures for Better Connections:

Mindfulness Practices: Recognize and address subliminal triggers that cause clashes or misconceptions.

Sympathy Representation: Use perception to envision yourself from someone else's perspective, cultivating more noteworthy empathy.

Assertions for Connections: Build up convictions like, "I draw in solid, adoring connections" or "I speak with clearness and benevolence."

Expanding Fearlessness

The psyche mind holds the way in to your mental self view. By reinventing it with positive convictions about your value and capacities, you can decisively build your certainty.

Moves toward Lift Certainty:

Day to day Certifications: "I'm sure and proficient" or "I merit achievement."

Envision Achievement: Envision yourself succeeding in circumstances where you normally feel unreliable.

Non-verbal communication Practices: Utilize certain stances and developments to flag confidence to your psyche.

Appreciation Reflection: Spotlight on your accomplishments and assets, regardless of how little, to overhaul your self-insight.

These applications feature how outfitting subliminal power can acquire significant changes various everyday issues.

Subliminal and Profound Wellbeing

The Connection Between Subliminal Examples and Feelings

The psyche mind is a supply of previous encounters, recollections, and learned ways of behaving, all of which fundamentally impact our profound wellbeing. Unsettled feelings, like apprehension, outrage, or trouble, frequently come from profoundly installed subliminal examples framed during youth or huge life altering situations.

For instance:

An individual with a subliminal conviction of dishonor may

regularly encounter sensations of nervousness or low confidence.

A positive subliminal relationship with confidence and backing cultivates versatility and close to home prosperity.

Understanding this connection is pivotal in light of the fact that profound reactions frequently work consequently, determined by subliminal programming. By recognizing and tending to these examples, you can make enduring profound equilibrium and recuperating.

Recuperating Through Subliminal Mindfulness

Recuperating close to home injuries starts with becoming mindful of subliminal triggers and examples. Close to home agony frequently continues on the grounds that the psyche mind clutches unsettled encounters or injury.

Methods to Advance Subliminal Profound Recuperating:

Care and Reflection: Customary care rehearses permit you to notice your feelings without judgment, assisting you with revealing psyche designs.

Journaling: Expounding on close to home encounters can carry subliminal contemplations to the surface, making them more clear and interaction.

Internal identity Work: Associating with your internal identity can mend subliminal injuries coming from early encounters. Envision consoling your more youthful self to deliver covered feelings.

Hypnotherapy: Spellbinding can get to the subliminal straightforwardly, assisting you with delivering profoundly installed close to home blocks.

Overseeing Pressure and Tension

Stress and tension are many times established in subliminal feelings of trepidation and convictions about the future or annoying issues from an earlier time. By tending to these hidden causes, you can reduce their effect on your profound wellbeing.

Moves toward Oversee Pressure and Uneasiness with Subliminal Work:

Reevaluate Negative Considerations: Supplant subliminal feelings of dread (e.g., "I will fizzle") with engaging assertions (e.g., "I have the solidarity to succeed").

Moderate Unwinding: Use unwinding methods like directed reflection or body examining to quiet the psyche and lessen nervousness.

Perception for Serenity: Envision a protected, quiet spot where you feel totally calm. Return to this psychological picture during unpleasant minutes.

Breathwork: Profound, deliberate breathing signs to the subliminal that you are protected, assisting with intruding on the pressure reaction.

Breaking the Pattern of Profound Triggers

Close to home triggers frequently originate from natural subliminal recollections. These triggers can make lopsided close to home responses certain circumstances, making it indispensable to break the cycle.

Moves toward Break the Cycle:

Recognize Triggers: Think about circumstances that reliably incite compelling profound responses.

Recognize the Underlying driver: Ask yourself, "What previous experience or conviction is filling this response?"

Reconstruct the Reaction: Use certifications, representation, or mental reevaluating to make a better reaction to the trigger.

Practice Persistence: Changing subliminal reactions takes time and steady exertion.

Building Close to home Strength

Close to home flexibility is the capacity to quickly return from difficulties. It's profoundly attached to subliminal convictions about your ability to deal with misfortune.

By reinforcing these convictions, you can develop a stronger mentality.

Ways Of building Close to home Flexibility:

Self-Attestation Practices: Routinely support convictions like, "areas of strength for i'm equipped for conquering difficulties."

Appreciation Activities: Spotlight on what you're grateful for to move your subliminal toward an uplifting perspective.

Perception of Accomplishment: Envision yourself effectively exploring tough spots to program flexibility into your psyche.

Flexibility Preparing: Open yourself to controlled changes or difficulties to show your subliminal that you can flourish in vulnerability.

Delivering Pessimistic Close to home Examples

Pessimistic profound examples, like displeasure, responsibility, or trouble, frequently become imbued in the subliminal because of redundancy. To deliver them, you want to make new, positive close to home affiliations.

Moves toward Delivery Negative Examples:

Recognize the Inclination: Stifling feelings just reinforces them. All things being equal, permit yourself to feel them completely without judgment.

Utilize Positive Anchors: Partner testing feelings with good improvements (e.g., quieting music or charming aromas) to make new subliminal associations.

Center around Absolution: Whether pardoning yourself or others, relinquishing disdain clears space in your subliminal for positive feelings.

Practice Profound Opportunity Methods (EFT): Tapping on pressure point massage focuses while zeroing in on gloomy feelings can assist with setting them free from the psyche.

By effectively working with your psyche mind, you can make enduring profound wellbeing, break liberated from restricting examples, and experience more noteworthy harmony and satisfaction.

Dreams and the Psyche

The Association Among Dreams and the Psyche Brain

Dreams are a door to the psyche mind, giving experiences into unsettled feelings, stowed away cravings, and firmly established convictions. During rest, when the cognizant psyche is very still, the inner mind turns out to be exceptionally dynamic, handling recollections, feelings, and encounters. Dreams frequently mirror this interaction, offering emblematic portrayals of our internal world.

The inner mind utilizes dreams to:

Process and coordinate everyday encounters.

Uncover unsettled clashes or stifled feelings.

Give innovative motivation or answers for issues.

While dreams could appear to be arbitrary or counter-intuitive, they are frequently profoundly associated with the functions of the inner mind, uncovering examples and messages that can direct self-awareness.

Sorts of Dreams and Their Subliminal Importance

Repeating Dreams

Repeating dreams demonstrate annoying issues or industrious

inner mind designs. These fantasies frequently feature fears, wants, or everyday issues that need consideration.

Model: Dreaming about being pursued could reflect evasion of a test or dread in cognizant existence.

Representative Dreams

The psyche frequently conveys in images and illustrations, making dream understanding an incredible asset for self-disclosure.

Model: A fantasy about water could represent feelings, with quiet water showing harmony and violent water addressing internal conflict.

Clear Dreams

In a clear dream, you know that you are dreaming and could handle the fantasy's heading. Clear dreaming furnishes a one of a kind chance to connect with the psyche mind and purposefully investigate its messages.

Bad dreams

Bad dreams are serious dreams that frequently come from unsettled fears or stress. They go about as the psyche brain's approach to encouraging you to go up against and address these issues.

Prophetic or Critical thinking Dreams

A few dreams seem to foresee occasions or give answers for issues. These may result from the psyche brain's capacity to deal with data and associate examples past the cognizant brain's ability.

Deciphering Dreams to Figure out the Inner mind

Keep a Fantasy Diary

Recording your fantasies quickly after waking assists you with catching their subtleties before they blur. Over the long run, designs and repeating images might arise, offering hints to subliminal subjects.

Recognize Images and Feelings

Search for key images in your fantasies and consider what they address in your life.

Focus on the feelings you felt during the fantasy, as they frequently reflect your subliminal sentiments about a circumstance.

Pose Inquiries About the Fantasy

Ponder the fantasy's account and inquire:

What parts of my cognizant existence does this fantasy connect with?

What message is my inner mind attempting to convey?

Are there unsettled feelings or fears the fantasy is featuring?

Look for Examples

On the off chance that specific topics or images repeat in your fantasies, they probably address annoying issues or critical parts of your psyche mind.

Utilizing Dreams to Saddle Subliminal Power

Set Goals Before Rest

Prior to hitting the sack, center around an inquiry or issue you'd like your subliminal to address. This training, known as "dream hatching," can direct your subliminal to give experiences during rest.

Model: Before rest, think, "How might I beat this test at work?" and notice on the off chance that your fantasies offer direction.

Practice Clear Dreaming

Clear dreaming permits you to communicate with your psyche mind while dreaming deliberately. Strategies to initiate clear dreaming include:

Rude awakenings: Over the course of the day, ask yourself, "Am I dreaming?" to assemble mindfulness.

Dream Signs: Distinguish repeating images or circumstances in your fantasies.

Reflection Before Rest: Loosen up your psyche to expand your possibilities of clarity.

Reflect on Dream Experiences

Subsequent to reviewing a fantasy, reflect on its images and feelings. This develops how you might interpret the subtle cues and how they connect with your cognizant existence.

Imagine Wanted Results in Dreams

Use representation methods to "program" your fantasies. Prior to rest, envision accomplishing an objective or settling an issue. Your psyche might handle this perception during the fantasy state, supporting your aims.

Dreams as a Way to Mending and Development

Dreams frequently uncover unsettled close to home injuries or restricting convictions that influence your cognizant existence. By investigating and tending to these subjects, you can mend subliminal examples and develop inwardly.

Ventures for Recuperating Through Dreams:

Recognize and Acknowledge: Perceive the fantasy as a message from your psyche and move toward it with interest, not dread or judgment.

Participate in Dynamic Creative mind: Use strategies like journaling or representation to proceed with the fantasy's account and look for goal.

Look for Proficient Direction: On the off chance that a fantasy features profound close to home agony or injury, working with a specialist can help unload and handle its significance.

Dreams are an incredible asset for getting to and figuring out the psyche mind. By focusing on your fantasies, you can open bits of knowledge, track down inventive motivation, and advance profound mending.

Instruments and Strategies to Bridle the Inner mind

The psyche mind works as a tremendous, strong component that can be taken advantage of and modified with the right devices and procedures. By intentionally working with it, you can overhaul restricting convictions, adjust your inward world to your objectives, and open your true capacity. The following are the absolute best strategies to access and bridle the psyche mind.

1. Perception

Perception includes making clear mental pictures of wanted results to program the psyche brain to pursue them.

Ventures for Powerful Perception:

Find a tranquil space where you will not be upset.

Shut your eyes and envision your objective as though it has previously been accomplished.

Utilize every one of your faculties: What do you see, hear, feel, and even smell in this situation?

Center around the feelings attached to accomplishing this objective (e.g., delight, pride, harmony).

Rehash the representation day to day, particularly in a casual state like before rest.

Benefits:

Supports inspiration and certainty.

Adjusts subliminal energy to cognizant objectives.

Initiates the mind's brain processes related with progress.

2. Certifications

Certifications are positive, current state explanations intended to supplant restricting convictions and build up engaging ones.

Instructions to Utilize Assertions:

Compose confirmations well defined for your objectives or areas of development (e.g., "I'm certain and proficient").

Rehash them out loud or quietly on various occasions everyday.

Utilize a mirror to make confirmations more effective by keeping in touch while talking them.

Practice insistences during loosened up states for better ingestion (e.g., during contemplation or just before rest).

Instances of Assertions:

"I draw in progress and overflow easily."

"I genuinely deserve love and regard."

"I'm strong and can conquer any test."

3. Reflection

Reflection is an incredible asset for calming the cognizant brain and getting to the psyche. It makes space for lucidity, understanding, and the reinventing of well established designs.

Strategies for Subliminal Access:

Care Reflection: Spotlight on your breath or substantial sensations to quiet the cognizant brain.

Directed Contemplation: Use sound tracks or applications with directed scripts zeroed in on unambiguous objectives, similar to certainty or mending.

Mantra Contemplation: Rehash a significant word or expression to moor your concentration and impact subliminal convictions.

Benefits:

Decreases mental babble, permitting subliminal examples to surface.

Improves profound equilibrium and versatility.

Further develops lucidity and spotlight on objectives.

4. Journaling

Composing connects with both the cognizant and subliminal personalities, making it a viable instrument for self-disclosure and development.

Journaling Procedures:

Continuous flow Composing: Compose whatever strikes a chord without judgment. This can uncover subliminal considerations and feelings.

Appreciation Journaling: Rundown things you're thankful for to reinvent the subliminal to zero in on overflow and energy.

Objective Journaling: Expound on your objectives as though they've proactively been accomplished, depicting the feelings and subtleties.

Dream Journaling: Record your fantasies after waking to investigate subliminal cues.

Benefits:

Uncovers stowed away convictions and feelings.

Fortifies center around sure parts of life.

Gives lucidity and bearing to self-improvement.

5. Hypnotherapy

Entrancing is a strategy to get to the psyche mind straight by inciting a profoundly loose, engaged state. In this express, the psyche turns out to be more open to ideas.

How It Functions:

A prepared subliminal specialist guides you into a daze like state, bypassing the basic cognizant psyche.

Positive ideas or certifications are acquainted with reconstruct restricting convictions or address explicit issues (e.g., nervousness, self-question).

Benefits:

Rapidly tends to well established subliminal examples.

Viable for defeating fears, building certainty, and bringing an end to propensities.

Can be self-directed through self-entrancing methods.

6. Subconscious Informing

Subconscious informing includes presenting the subliminal to positive confirmations or viewable signs that sidestep the cognizant brain.

Techniques for Subconscious Programming:

Sound Tracks: Pay attention to attestations implanted in loosening up music or background noise.

Viewable Prompts: Use vision sheets or compose confirmations where you'll see them everyday (e.g., tacky notes on a mirror).

Applications and Innovation: Numerous applications offer subconscious sound tracks custom fitted to different objectives.

Benefits:

Reconstructs the subliminal without dynamic exertion.

Supports positive convictions over the long haul.

Viable for propensity building and attitude shifts.

7. Close to home Opportunity Strategies (EFT)

Otherwise called "tapping," EFT includes tapping on pressure point massage focuses while zeroing in on unambiguous feelings or convictions.

Instructions to Utilize EFT:

Distinguish the issue you need to address (e.g., apprehension about disappointment).

Utilize an arrangement proclamation, for example, "Despite the fact that I feel [emotion], I profoundly and totally acknowledge myself."

Tap on unambiguous focuses (e.g., side of the hand, under the eye, top of the head) while rehashing insistences or zeroing in on the issue.

Benefits:

Discharges profound blocks put away in the psyche.

Quiets pressure and nervousness.

Supports positive convictions and self-acknowledgment.

8. Innovative Perception Through Vision Sheets

Vision sheets are a visual portrayal of your objectives and wants. They act as an amazing asset to impart your goals to the psyche mind.

Step by step instructions to Make a Dream Board:

Assemble pictures, statements, and images that address your objectives.

Organize them on a board or computerized material.

Place the vision board where you'll see it day to day to build up subliminal concentration.

Benefits:

Keeps your objectives top-of-mind.

Supports confidence in accomplishing wanted results.

Fortifies close to home association with your desires.

9. Reiteration and Propensity Development

The inner mind learns through reiteration. By more than once presenting the brain to positive propensities, convictions, or activities, you can reconstruct it after some time.

Strategies:

Lay out day to day ceremonies lined up with your objectives (e.g., working out, reflecting, or attesting achievement).

Use updates or propensity following applications to keep up with consistency.

Match new propensities with existing schedules (e.g., confirmations during your morning espresso).

Benefits:

Fortifies brain processes related with wanted ways of behaving.

Builds up sure convictions and propensities.

Advances long haul subliminal programming.

10. Appreciation Practices

Appreciation is a high-recurrence feeling that straightforwardly impacts the psyche mind. Routinely zeroing in on what you're thankful for shifts your mentality from shortage to overflow.

Appreciation Procedures:

Record three things you're appreciative for every day.

Consider positive minutes before bed to establish a thankful vibe for your subliminal during rest.

Offer thanks so anyone might hear or to others to support the inclination.

Benefits:

Upgrades close to home prosperity.

Fortifies positive subliminal affiliations.

Draws in additional energy and overflow into your life.

Bridling the psyche mind requires reliable practice, persistence, and deliberateness. By consolidating these devices and strategies, you can open the colossal capability of your subliminal to change your life.

Contextual investigations and Genuine Models

Genuine uses of subliminal brain methods exhibit their groundbreaking likely in different parts of life. The following are instances of people and situations where tackling the psyche mind prompted momentous results.

1. Defeating Self-Uncertainty to Make Proficient Progress

Contextual analysis:

Emma, a Promoting Director

Challenge: Emma battled with persistent self-uncertainty and an inability to embrace success, feeling shameful of advancements in spite of her capabilities.

Subliminal Methods Utilized:

Emma began an everyday confirmation work on, rehashing, "I'm certain, competent, and meriting achievement."

She pictured herself succeeding in gatherings, getting acknowledgment, and driving activities with certainty.

She additionally journaled about her achievements to build up her self-esteem.

Result: In something like a half year, Emma saw a critical change in her certainty. She applied for an influential position, aced the meeting, and was advanced. Her newly discovered self-conviction made her a more powerful and regarded pioneer.

2. Mending from Injury Through Subliminal Reinventing

Contextual investigation:

John, a Veteran

Challenge: John experienced repeating bad dreams and uneasiness because of unsettled injury from his tactical assistance.

Subliminal Strategies Utilized:

John worked with a subliminal specialist to return to and rethink horrible recollections in a protected and strong setting.

He rehearsed Close to home Opportunity Methods (EFT) to

deliver profound pressure and diminish nervousness triggers.

Through directed contemplation, he imagined a serene future and bit by bit supplanted dread with trust.

Result: After some time, John's bad dreams reduced, and his tension became reasonable. He discovered a sense of harmony in his day to day existence and started imparting his story to rouse others to comparative encounters.

3. Accomplishing Athletic Greatness with Perception

Contextual investigation:

Michael Phelps, Olympic Swimmer

Challenge: Contending at the most significant level required actual preparation as well as mental arrangement.

Subliminal Methods Utilized:

Phelps pictured each race exhaustively, envisioning himself executing wonderful strokes, turns, and wraps up.

He rehearsed mental practices to plan for startling difficulties, similar to a goggle breakdown.

Positive confirmations, for example, "I'm solid, centered, and relentless," were important for his pre-race schedule.

Result: Phelps turned into the most improved Olympian ever, with his representation methods credited as a foundation of his prosperity.

4. Changing Monetary Outlook to Create Financial momentum

Contextual investigation:

Lisa, a Business person

Challenge: Lisa confronted monetary battles right off the bat in her business and accepted she was "terrible with cash," a restricting subliminal conviction she had acquired from her childhood.

Subliminal Methods Utilized:

Lisa stood by listening to subconscious assertions like, "I draw in riches and overflow easily," while working.

She made a dream board displaying monetary objectives, for example, obligation free living and worldwide business development.

Appreciation journaling assisted her shift with centering to the monetary successes, regardless of how little, fabricating an overflow attitude.

Result: In no less than two years, Lisa's business developed fundamentally. She defeated her feeling of dread toward monetary administration, employed a mentor, and accomplished her monetary achievements, including buying her most memorable home.

5. Imaginative Leap forward Through Subliminal Investigation

Contextual analysis:

Salvador Dalí, Surrealist Painter

Challenge: Dalí tried to make craftsmanship that took advantage of more profound, illusory conditions of the inner mind.

Subliminal Methods Utilized:

Dalí rehearsed "hypnagogic dreaming," where he would nod off holding a key. At the point when the key dropped, the sound would wake him, permitting him to catch distinctive subliminal symbolism.

He utilized free affiliation and journaling to catch dream images and feelings.

Result: Dalí's works of art, for example, "The Perseverance of Memory," became famous portrayals of the psyche mind in workmanship. His strategies are currently broadly contemplated and celebrated.

6. Getting out from under Habit-forming Propensities Through Subliminal Overhauling

Contextual investigation:

Mark, a Previous Smoker

Challenge: Imprint had smoked for a long time and battled with desires even after a few bombed endeavors to stop.

Subliminal Procedures Utilized:

Mark worked with a trance inducer who utilized directed ideas to reevaluate his relationship with smoking, partner it with inconvenience instead of unwinding.

He utilized representation, envisioning himself solid, lively, and liberated from smoking.

Day to day confirmations like, "I'm in charge of my wellbeing," fortified his purpose.

Result: Imprint effectively quit smoking following three months of subliminal reinventing. He revealed feeling engaged and more grounded than at any other time.

7. Working on Profound Flexibility with Contemplation

Contextual investigation:

Sophia, a Teacher

Challenge: Sophia frequently felt overpowered by her responsibility and battled to adjust her obligations.

Subliminal Methods Utilized:

Sophia rehearsed care contemplation to quiet her psyche and interface with her inward strength.

Appreciation journaling helped her emphasis on the up-sides in her day, reexamining her mentality from stress to appreciation.

She utilized moderate unwinding strategies to loosen up before bed, lessening subliminal pressure.

Result: In no time, Sophia felt more grounded and fit for dealing with her responsibility. Her superior close to home flexibility permitted her to completely partake in her profession and individual life more.

8. Helping Scholastic Execution Through Attestations

Contextual investigation:

David, an Undergrad

Challenge: David battled with test nervousness, prompting horrible showing in spite of his planning.

Subliminal Procedures Utilized:

He made certifications like, "I'm quiet, sure, and centered during tests."

David envisioned himself going into the test room, feeling quiet and addressing inquiries easily.

He working on breathing procedures to loosen up his body

and calm his psyche prior to contemplating and tests.

Result: David's uneasiness lessened, and his exhibition improved altogether. He graduated with distinction and credited his psyche work for his scholarly circle back.

Key Focus points from These Models

Steady Practice Is Fundamental: Genuine change requires ordinary use of subliminal methods.

Consolidating Techniques Yields Improved Results: Numerous fruitful people utilize a blend of representation, insistences, reflection, and different instruments.

The Inner mind Answers Energy: Supplanting restricting convictions with engaging ones is a foundation of progress.

Proficient Direction Can Speed up Results: Hypnotherapy or instructing can extend subliminal work for explicit difficulties.

Challenges in Working with the Psyche

Taking advantage of and reinventing the psyche mind is a groundbreaking interaction, however it accompanies its own arrangement of difficulties. These impediments frequently come from profoundly instilled convictions, routine reasoning examples, or protection from change. Understanding these difficulties can assist you with exploring them all the more successfully and remain focused on your development.

1. Well established Restricting Convictions

Challenge:

Many restricting convictions are imbued during youth and work underneath cognizant mindfulness, forming insights, choices, and ways of behaving. These convictions can feel like unchangeable insights, making them hard to recognize and supplant.

Model:

An individual raised to accept "Cash is the foundation of all shrewd" could subliminally damage monetary achievement, in any event, when they deliberately want riches.

Arrangement:

Utilize self-reflection, journaling, or treatment to reveal stowed away convictions.

Practice insistences and representation to supplant these convictions with engaging ones.

Show restraint; well established convictions frequently get some margin to move.

2. Protection from Change

Challenge:

The psyche mind is intended to keep up with consistency and shield you from saw gambles. Accordingly, it frequently opposes change, regardless of whether the change is useful.

Model:

Somebody attempting to embrace a better way of life might battle with old propensities in light of the fact that their psyche partners solace with natural schedules.

Arrangement:

Begin with little, reasonable changes to diminish opposition.

Use reiteration to construct new propensities and brain connections after some time.

Recognize opposition as a feature of the cycle and help yourself to remember your objectives.

3. Absence of Mindfulness

Challenge:

Since the psyche mind works behind the scenes, many individuals know nothing about its impact on their viewpoints, feelings, and ways of behaving. This absence of mindfulness can thwart progress.

Model:

An individual might battle with repeating relationship designs without acknowledging they come from subliminal feelings of dread or convictions about self-esteem.

Arrangement:

Practice care to increment mindfulness and notice thought designs.

Focus on triggers, dreams, or repeating ways of behaving as hints to subliminal programming.

Look for direction from books, studios, or experts having some expertise in subliminal work.

4. Profound Blocks

Challenge:

Compelling feelings like apprehension, responsibility, disgrace, or outrage can impede admittance to the psyche mind and forestall viable reinventing.

Model:

An individual conveying culpability from a previous oversight may subliminally stay away from progress or joy, it are undeserving to trust they.

Arrangement:

Utilize Close to home Opportunity Procedures (EFT) or reflection to deliver profound strain.

Look for restorative techniques like hypnotherapy or guiding to process and determine profound blocks.

Center around self-sympathy and absolution to recuperate gloomy feelings.

5. Overthinking and Mental Babble

Challenge:

The cognizant psyche frequently overanalyzes or questions the most common way of working with the inner mind, prompting mental jabber that disturbs concentration and progress.

Model:

While rehearsing attestations, somebody could think, "This isn't working," or "I don't completely accept that this," sabotaging the work.

Arrangement:

Practice contemplation to calm the cognizant psyche and access further conditions of unwinding.

Center around sentiments as opposed to rationale while utilizing procedures like representation.

Trust the cycle and advise yourself that subliminal programming requires some investment.

6. Eagerness with Results

Challenge:

The psyche mind works step by step, frequently requiring weeks or long stretches of predictable work to deliver recognizable changes. This can prompt disappointment or surrendering rashly.

Model:

An individual attempting to show monetary accomplishment through representation might become dispirited following half a month without noticeable outcomes.

Arrangement:

Set practical assumptions and spotlight on little, steady changes.

Keep tabs on your development to remain roused and perceive unpretentious movements.

Recall that consistency is critical, and leap forwards frequently happen out of the blue.

7. Clashing Longings

Challenge:

Cognizant objectives and subliminal programming might struggle, making inside strain and destructive behavior.

Model:

Somebody could intentionally need a caring relationship yet subliminally dread weakness because of past heartbreaks.

Arrangement:

Use journaling or treatment to investigate and accommodate clashing cravings.

Practice mindfulness to recognize and address fears or questions.

Center around adjusting your cognizant and subliminal objectives through predictable practice.

8. Misapplication of Strategies

Challenge:

Ill-advised utilization of subliminal apparatuses can decrease their adequacy or even support restricting convictions.

Model:

Rehashing attestations without profound association might neglect to impact the inner mind.

Arrangement:

Learn appropriate strategies through books, courses, or expert direction.

Connect completely with techniques like representation, certifications, or reflection by zeroing in on feelings and tangible subtleties.

Tailor strategies to your own inclinations and objectives.

9. Outer Impacts and Negative Molding

Challenge:

Outer impacts, like cultural assumptions, media, or unsupportive conditions, can support restricting convictions or occupy from subliminal work.

Model:

Somebody attempting to construct self-assurance might battle whenever encompassed by basic or pessimistic individuals.

Arrangement:

Limit openness to adverse impacts and encircle yourself with steady, similar people.

Use devices like certifications and appreciation journaling to balance outside pessimism.

Make a positive, objective situated climate that builds up your psyche work.

10. Anxiety toward the Unexplored world

Challenge:

Investigating the psyche brain can uncover stowed away feelings, recollections, or convictions that might feel awkward or overpowering.

Model:

During contemplation, somebody might review a difficult youth experience they hadn't intentionally recalled.

Arrangement:

Move toward subliminal work with interest and a non-critical disposition.

Look for help from a specialist or tutor in the event that you uncover troublesome feelings or recollections.

Center around the drawn out advantages of self-revelation and recuperating.

Conquering the Difficulties

While these difficulties might appear to be overwhelming, they are essential for the course of development and change. By developing tolerance, consistency, and self-sympathy, you can manage these deterrents and open the huge capability of your psyche mind.

End

The psyche mind holds uncommon power, significantly shaping our contemplations, convictions, feelings, and activities in significant ways. While frequently underrated, it is the groundwork of individual change and a vital aspect for opening boundless potential. By figuring out its operations, tending to difficulties, and applying demonstrated methods, we can reinvent our psyche brain to line up with our cognizant objectives, making an existence of satisfaction, achievement, and profound prosperity.

The excursion into the inner mind is both a test and an open door. It requires tolerance, perseverance, and an eagerness to stand up to secret feelings of dread and restricting convictions. However, the prizes — more prominent mindfulness, profound versatility, and the capacity to show positive results — merit the work. Whether through certifications, perception, contemplation, or different devices, the most common way of working with the inner mind engages us to break liberated from old examples and make a reality lined up with our most elevated yearnings.

At last, the psyche mind is an extension between what our identity is and who we wish to turn into. By bridling its power with goal and lucidity, we can change our own lives as well as rouse people around us to do likewise. The potential is boundless — what we accept, we genuinely can accomplish.

www.ingramcontent.com/pod-product-compliance
Lightning Source LLC
Chambersburg PA
CBHW050324230526
45471CB00005B/2336